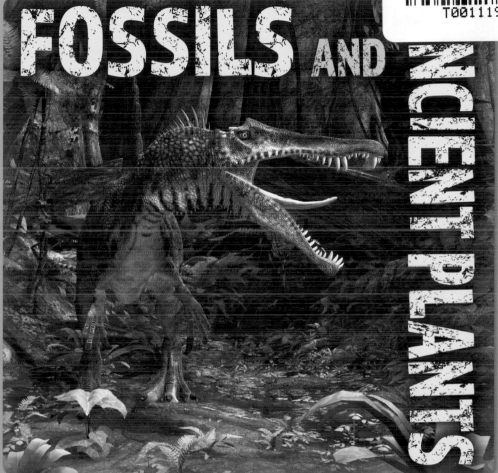

FOSSILS AND ANCIENT PLANTS

by Kelli Hicks

A Crabtree Seedlings Book

CRABTREE
Publishing Company
www.crabtreebooks.com

Paleontology (pay-lee-uhn-TOL-uh-jee):
the study of ancient life using fossils

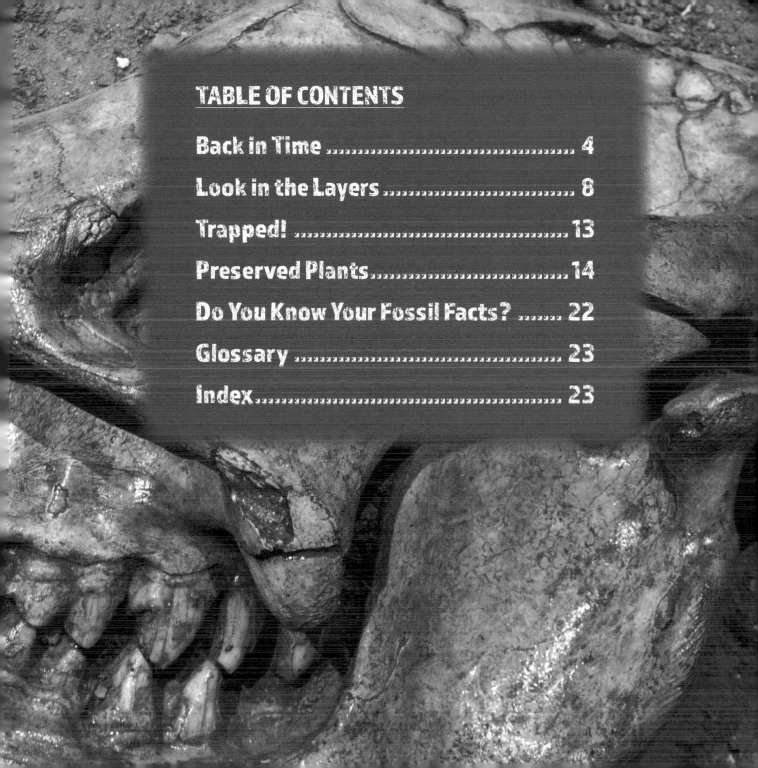

TABLE OF CONTENTS

Back in Time

Imagine a time when dinosaurs roamed Earth.

Can you see the long-necked Apatosaurus *(uh-paa-tuh-saw-ruhs)? It ate ancient ferns and other plants.*

Ceratosaurus *(ser-at-o-saw-ruhs)*
was a meat-eater.

How do we know about
these animals? We know
from finding **fossils**.

Fossils give us information about animals that lived millions of years ago. **Paleontologists** study fossils to learn about the history of living and extinct **organisms**.

*Body fossils are parts of the organism, such as bones or teeth. **Imprints** left in rock are called trace fossils.*

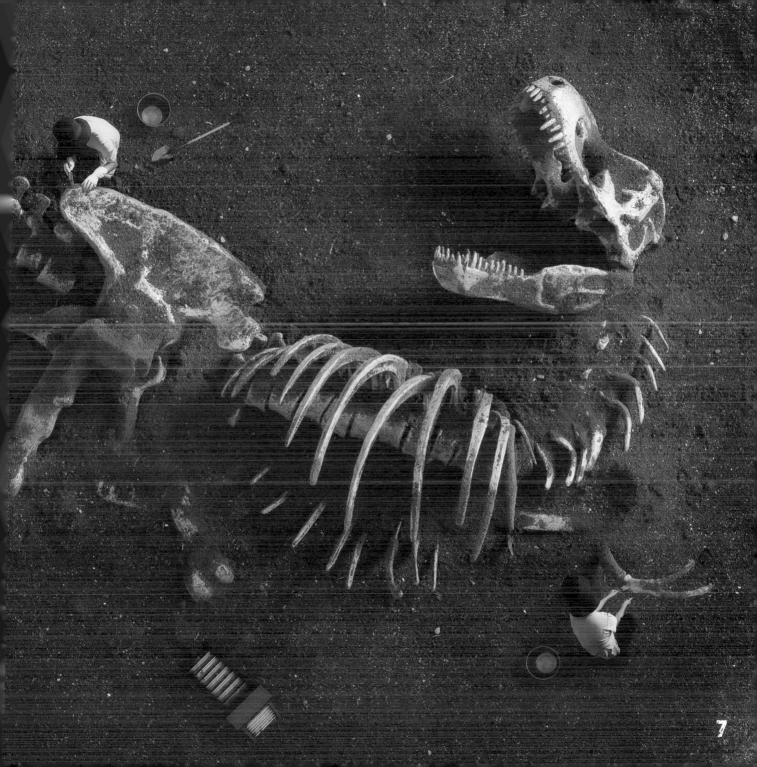

Look in the Layers

Fossils form in different ways. When an animal in nature dies, the body of the animal begins to **decompose**.

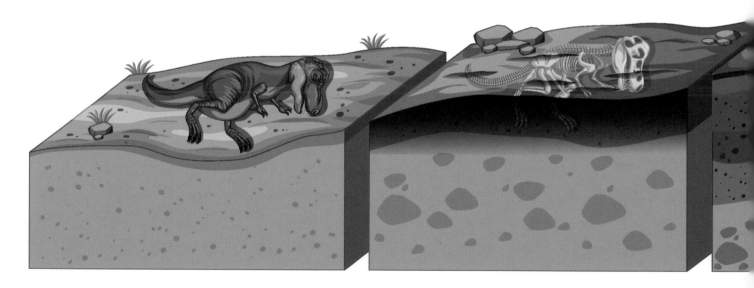

The soft parts of the organism rot and dissolve into the soil.

Over time, muscles and tissues break down and get buried under layers of dirt, called **sediment**.

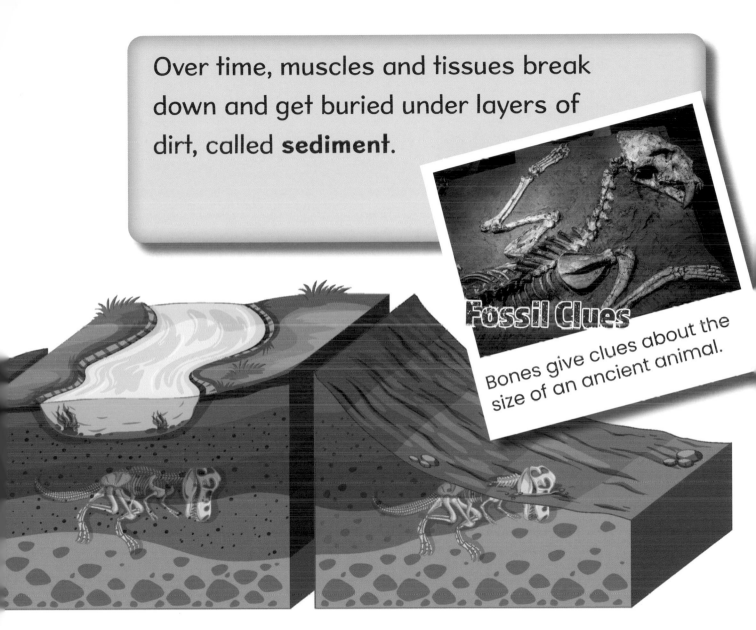

Fossil Clues

Bones give clues about the size of an ancient animal.

The harder parts, such as bones and teeth, stay behind in the sediment and the fossil forms.

Some animals make imprints in soft materials, such as mud. Over time, the wet mud dries out and hardens into rock.

Scientists have found fossils formed from dinosaur footprints left in the mud millions of years ago.

Fossil Clues

Dinosaur tracks give information about how fast the dinosaur moved, its size, if it had two or four feet, and if it traveled in groups.

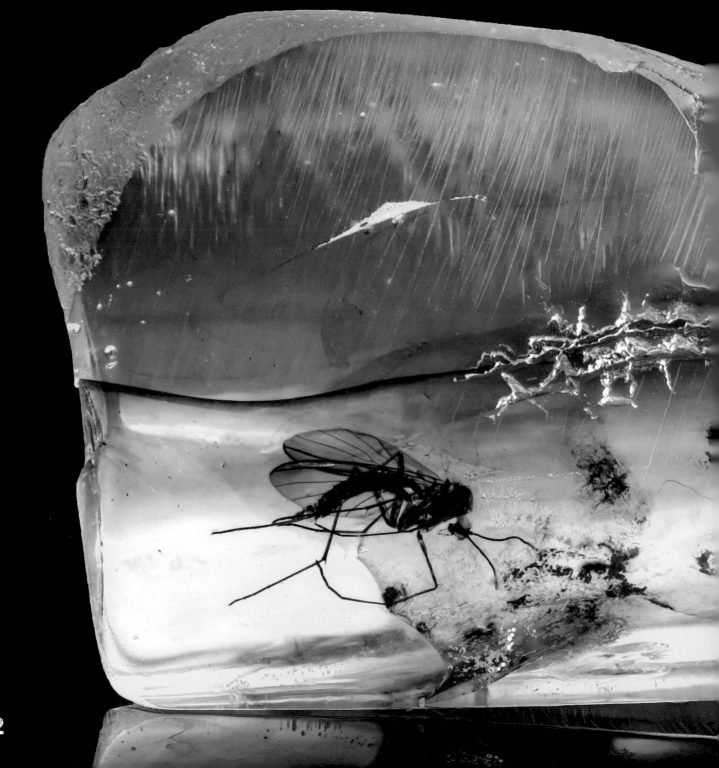

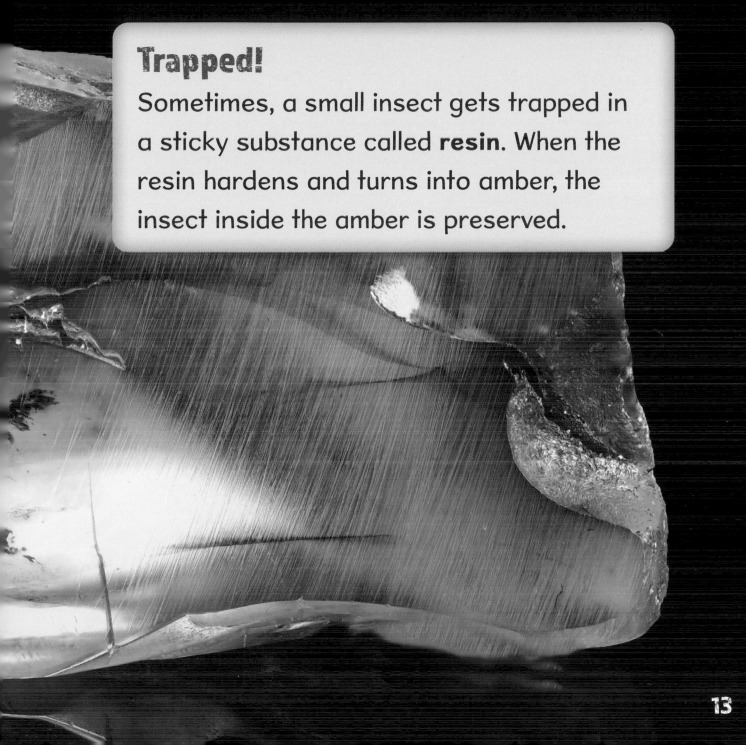

Trapped!

Sometimes, a small insect gets trapped in a sticky substance called **resin**. When the resin hardens and turns into amber, the insect inside the amber is preserved.

Preserved Plants

Animals aren't the only living things that can leave an imprint as a fossil. Plants and plant pieces can fossilize as well.

There are ancient plants, such as the Wollemi Pine, that scientists can trace back to the time of the dinosaurs.

Fossil records show that the Wollemi Pine is one of the world's oldest plants.

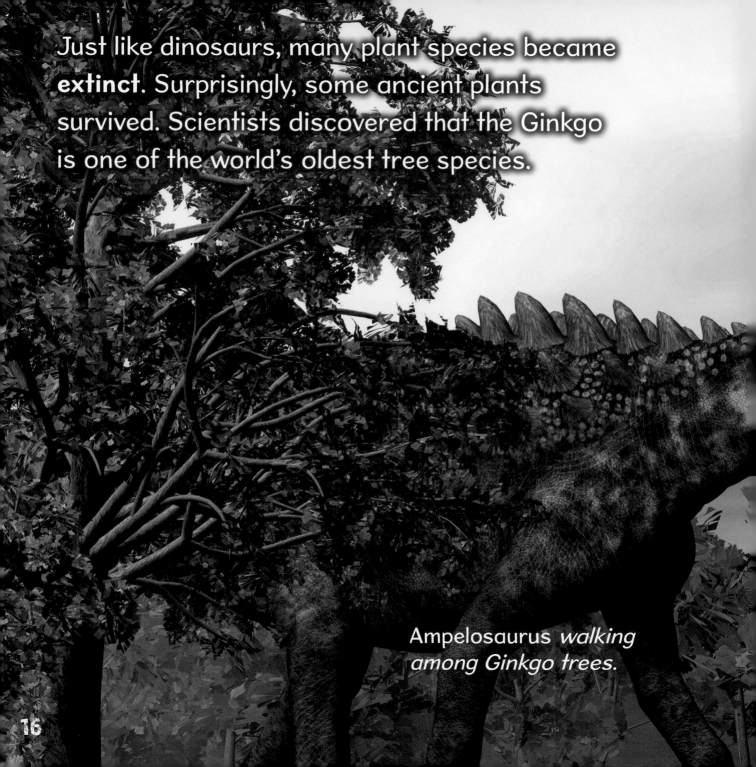

Just like dinosaurs, many plant species became **extinct**. Surprisingly, some ancient plants survived. Scientists discovered that the Ginkgo is one of the world's oldest tree species.

Ampelosaurus *walking among Ginkgo trees.*

Because it has barely changed, scientists call the Ginkgo tree a "living fossil."

Petrified wood is a fossil. It forms
when plant material or a fallen tree
gets buried under layers of sediment.

*Visitors can see the many colors of petrified
wood at Petrified Forest National Park in Arizona.*

Groundwater, rich in minerals, flows into the sediment and replaces the original plant material with a hard substance called **silica**.

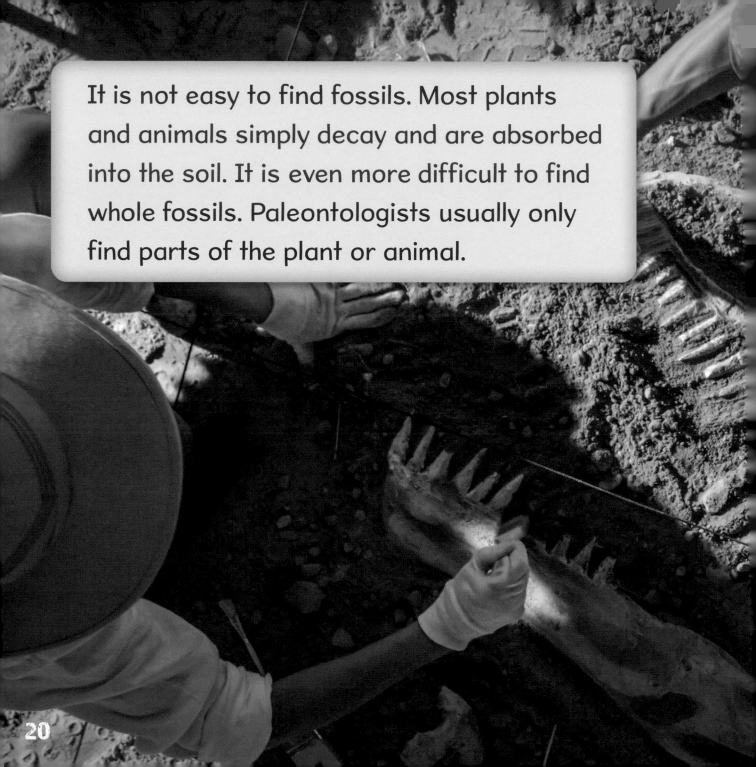

It is not easy to find fossils. Most plants and animals simply decay and are absorbed into the soil. It is even more difficult to find whole fossils. Paleontologists usually only find parts of the plant or animal.

Fossil Clues

Scientists can learn about dinosaurs by studying fossilized poop called coprolites. They can find out if the dinosaur was a meat-eater or a plant-eater.

DO YOU KNOW YOUR FOSSIL FACTS?

1. How do fossils form?
a. Plant or animal material gets left behind in layers of sediment
b. Plant or animal material decomposes
c. Rushing water moves plant or animal material into the river

2. What is a "living fossil"?
a. An animal that lives in resin
b. A plant or animal that has changed little over time
c. A plant or animal that is extinct

3. What forms when a fallen tree gets buried under layers of sediment, then gets covered in mineral-rich water, and hardens into silica?
a. Petrified wood
b. A living fossil
c. Resin

Answers:
1. a
2. b
3. a

Glossary

decompose (DEE-kuhm-poze): To rot or decay

fossils (FOSS-uhlz): The remains or traces of an animal or plant from millions of years ago, preserved in rock

imprints (IM-printz): Marks made by pressing on a surface

organisms (OR-guh-niz-uhmz): Living plants or animals

paleontologists (PAY-lee-un-TOL-uh-jists): Scientists who study fossils and other ancient life-forms

petrified (PE-truh-fide): Something that has slowly changed into stone or a stony substance over a long period of time

resin (REZ-in): A yellow or brown sticky substance that oozes from certain trees and plants

sediment (SED-uh-muhnt): Rocks, sand, or dirt that has been carried to a place by water, wind, or a glacier

silica (SIL-i-kuh): A compound that consists of dioxide and silicon that occurs in various forms, such as in quartz, opal, and sand

Index

School-to-Home Support for Caregivers and Teachers

This book helps children grow by letting them practice reading. Here are a few guiding questions to help the reader build his or her comprehension skills. Possible answers appear here in red.

Before Reading

- **What do I think this book is about?** I think this book is about fossils and ancient plants. I think this book is about trees that lived a very long time ago.

- **What do I want to learn about this topic?** I want to learn more about what types of plants were on Earth when the dinosaurs were alive. I want to learn how scientists find fossils.

During Reading

- **I wonder why...** I wonder why there are only a few types of trees still here that were around in ancient times. I wonder why so many other types of ancient trees died off.

- **What have I learned so far?** I have learned that when a small insect gets trapped in a sticky substance called resin it is preserved forever. I have learned that scientists have found fossils formed from dinosaur footprints left in the mud millions of years ago.

After Reading

- **What details did I learn about this topic?** I have learned that scientists can learn about dinosaurs by studying fossilized poop. I have learned that scientists can determine if the dinosaur was a meat-eater or a plant-eater by studying dinosaur poop.

- **Read the book again and look for the glossary words.** I see the word *resin* on page 13, and the word *silica* on page 19. The other glossary words are found on page 23.

Library and Archives Canada Cataloguing in Publication

CIP available at Library and Archives Canada

Library of Congress Cataloging-in-Publication Data

CIP available at Library of Congress

Crabtree Publishing Company

www.crabtreebooks.com   1–800–387–7650

Written by: Kelli Hicks

Production coordinator and Prepress technician: Tammy McGarr

Print coordinator: Katherine Berti

Print book version produced jointly with Blue Door Education in 2022

Printed in the U.S.A./CG20210915/012022

PHOTO CREDITS:
Cover © Valentyna Chukhlyebova, Pages 2-3 © Alizada Studios, Page 4 © Herschel Hoffmeyer, page 5 © DM7, pages 6-7 © Rafael Trafaniuc, inset photo of trilobites © Abrilla, page 8-9 illustration © BlueRingMedia, page 10 © Joaquin Corbalan P, page 11 large photo © Puwadol Jaturawutthichai, inset photo © Rattana, page 12-13 © RomanVX, back cover and page 14-15 large photo © Nuntiya, inset of Wollemi Pine © Dorothy Chiron, page 16-17 main image © Elenarts, Inset pic of Gingko © Anna L. e Marina Durante, page 18-19 © Juan Carlos Munoz, inset photo page 19 © Alex Coan, page 21 coprolites © Alex Coan. All images from Shutterstock.com except pages 20-21 paleontologists © gorodenkoff | istockphoto

Published in the United States
Crabtree Publishing
347 Fifth Ave.
Suite 1402-145
New York, NY 10016

Published in Canada
Crabtree Publishing
616 Welland Ave.
St. Catharines, Ontario
L2M 5V6